ENDORSEMENTS

I have had the pleasure of knowing Pastor Marshall Townsley for more than 35 years. His understanding of Scripture and how to apply it to our lives is inspiring! I wholeheartedly encourage everyone who is serious about growing in their relationship and walk with God to read and study his new book about how Psalm 23 relates to our lives. You will be grateful!

Pastor Charles Nieman
Abundant Church
El Paso, Texas

In Matthew 16:18, Jesus promised to build His Church on the rock—the revelation knowledge of who He is. This rock of revelation is the foundation on which we are called to build our lives. In Luke 4:18-20, we see the sermon Jesus preached from Isaiah, where He declared that He was anointed to preach the gospel. In Ephesians 4:11-12, Paul tells us that Jesus gave gifts to the Church to equip the saints for ministry.

Pastor Marshall Townsley is one of God's chosen servants, anointed as both pastor and teacher. He is anointed to preach the gospel just as Jesus was. A distinctive aspect of Marshall's ministry is the depth of his revelation, which enriches his teaching. His commentary on the 23rd Psalm exemplifies his love for Scripture and the profound insights the Holy Spirit has revealed to him from this Psalm. Through this work, he equips believers to know and understand Jesus as our beloved Shepherd and His unwavering love and care for His Church.

Thank you, Pastor Marshall, for your dedication in writing this book and for being a godly example as both Christian and pastor-teacher.

Don Caywood, Pastor
Odessa Christian Faith Center
Odessa, Texas

Pastor Marshall Townsley is one of the best teachers in the body of Christ. The revelation, given to him by the Holy Spirit, is always taught in a practical and applicable way. This is true of his book, *The Power of the 23rd Psalm.*

This cherished psalm is quoted more often than any other. But Pastor Marshall has written for us a masterpiece of practical wisdom that can be applied to our lives every day. King David wrote this psalm during a very troubling period of time in his own life, a time of pain, hurt, confusion, and chaos. Psalm 23 was his hope and faith in God, and Pastor Marshall has put it in a perspective that we all can relate to and need on a daily basis. This book will help you get through and overcome any unexpected circumstances that challenge your faith. It will bring you faith, hope, and peace in the middle of your storm. It will bring comfort and assurance to you as you walk through times of intense instability. It is a must read!

Pastor Al Brice
Covenant Love Church
Fayetteville, North Carolina

THE POWER OF THE 23rd Psalm

THE POWER OF THE 23rd Psalm

HIS PRESENCE, PROTECTION, AND PROVISION FOR YOUR JOURNEY OF FAITH

MARSHALL TOWNSLEY

All emphasis within Scripture quotations is the author's own.

Published by Harrison House Publishers
Shippensburg, PA 17257

ISBN 13 TP: 978-1-6675-1202-0
ISBN 13 eBook: 978-1-6675-1203-7

For Worldwide Distribution, Printed in the U.S.A.
1 2 3 4 5 6 7 8 / 29 28 27 26 25

DEDICATION

Cindi, my wife—My forever love in life, marriage and ministry. No one has ever graced my life more.

Hannah and Jordan, my girls—What as inspiration you both are! The favor of loving you is only surpassed by the favor of being loved by you.

Garry, my brother—Your love and loyalty have humbled me. The way you steward your gifts inspire. And your willingness to partner with me in the Gospel leave me speechless.

Kaye Mountz—I express my gratitude for your professional yet friendly approach to helping me give birth to and complete this project. Your positive attitude and dedication kept me motivated and inspired to share this message with all those who need it. I genuinely feel like I've made a new friend whom I can trust and respect moving forward. Thank you, again, for everything!

The team at Harrison House—I have admired your work for decades. I am in awe at your willingness and dedication to carry forward the original vision to publish and promote the Spirit-filled and abundant life Jesus has graced us with. You have always carried a spirit of excellence in all you do, and I am indebted to you for your decision to promote this version of *The Power of the 23rd Psalm*.

CONTENTS

FOREWORD

by Andrew Wommack

Marshall has not only been a great friend of mine since the 1970s, he's also a very powerful minister who has touched the lives of tens of thousands of people. His decades of ministry experience and study in the Word of God are reflected in this unique commentary on the 23rd Psalm.

Like all of Scripture, there are layers or depths of God's Word that have to be peeled back and mined to reap the real treasures that lie within. Marshall has dealt with every word and phrase of this psalm in such a way that you will gain new insight into our awesome

Shepherd whom David was describing in this beautiful song of praise.

Marshall first paraphrases this whole psalm expounding on its truths in ways that apply directly to us in our everyday lives. Then he goes back through each word or phrase in depth, commenting on the Hebrew meanings of words, the names of God, bringing other scriptures to bear, and giving historical context to the way shepherding was done to make these verses come alive.

I know you will find this short, easy-to-read commentary a valuable resource in relating to the Lord on a more intimate level. I have personally seen the Lord sustain Marshall through many trials, and these same truths that have brought him comfort and victory will work for you.

The Lord loves each one of us more than we can possibly imagine, but that doesn't mean we shouldn't try to know Him even more. This book will help bring you a little closer to experiencing the unfathomable riches of God's love.

Andrew Wommack
Founder and President
Andrew Wommack Ministries
and Charis Bible College

FOREWORD

by Rick Renner

It is my honor to write this foreword for my dear friend, Marshall Townsley, who has authored this heartfelt commentary about the 23rd Psalm. The subtitle of his book, *The Power of the 23rd Psalm,* says that by reading this, you will learn about God's presence, God's protection, and God's provision for your journey of faith. Since each of us needs the presence, protection, and provision of God, I was ready to dive in to see how this book would especially speak to my own heart.

I have always cherished the 23rd Psalm. But as I read this book, I realized that Marshall marvelously decided to deal with the entire psalm by covering every word, phrase, and nuance separately. Step by step, point by point, Marshall has provided wonderful insights to each word and phrase in Psalm 23. As a lover of God's Word, I took time to carefully read every comment and insight, and I found it to be nourishing to my own heart and spirit as I did. I know it will be a source of nourishment for you as well.

In addition to commenting on the 23rd Psalm, Marshall also weaves into his writing commentary on various titles of God in the Old Testament, the protection provided to those who live in the shadow of the Almighty, the ministry of the Holy Spirit, and the unfathomable and divine love God has for each of His children.

From the first word to the last, I found this easy-to-read book encouraging, and I am confident it will thrill the heart of any person who cries out to know God more intimately. What I also like is that it is a short read that can be read in a single sitting.

This book, *The Power of the 23rd Psalm,* is very impactful to the heart and strengthening, so I encourage you to take the time, as I did, to carefully read every word in it, because it has been carefully crafted for your edification. As the subtitle says, this book is intended to help you know and experience God's presence, protection, and provision in your own life.

I am thankful to Marshall for writing it!

Rick Renner
Author, Teacher, Pastor, Broadcaster
Moscow, Russia

INTRODUCTION

Like so many other believers, I love this psalm of David.

The revelation and understanding it offers about the Good Shepherd's presence, protection, and provision are as relevant today as when they were first penned. Its impact is as strong today as at any time in history for all who are familiar with it.

This beautiful psalm is loaded with great nuggets of truth lying beneath the surface of those familiar verses many believers have read so often. Six verses in the middle of our Bibles that have comforted, sustained, and encouraged us both in times of faith and fear and seasons of plenty and little.

I am deeply indebted to W. Phillip Keller whose book *A Shepherd Looks at Psalm 23* helped to deepen my own understanding of the culture surrounding the tedious work and constant challenges facing a shepherd and his sheep. As a Christian and a shepherd, his insights were not only indispensable but trustworthy in forming a solid foundation for this book and the interpretive version of the 23rd Psalm that I have provided for you.

The publishers and I have provided you a traditional copy of the 23rd Psalm to read first. You may have read it countless times or this may be the first time you've ever actually seen it in print. Whatever the case, it is an unmatched account of the celebrated relationship between the shepherd and his sheep—the Good Shepherd, Jesus, and those who follow Him in life. All Scripture is inspired or breathed out by God. His voice print rests upon it. You should expect as you simply read it, before you dig in to study it, to be blessed and refreshed. The writer of the book of Hebrews could only describe it as "alive" (Hebrews 4:12).

Then as you are ready, dive in and enjoy the interpretive version that the Spirit of God gave me. An interpretive version offers a little more than a simple paraphrase not only preserving the same idea as the original text but providing context, theology in this case, as well as some personal insight.

I've also included what I chose to call "Grazing Points." I encourage you to spend a little extra time thinking and meditating on these points. Some are brief enough you may even want to memorize them. One of the primary ways we get rooted in God's Word is to meditate or think on it. Our minds are in desperate need of renovation. And we are urged in Scripture to experience transformation by the renewing—not removing— of our minds! (Romans 12:1-2)

Traditionally, the 23rd Psalm is applied in times of deep sorrow or great loss—and rightly so. However, this heartfelt song written by King David reminds us that God's love for us covers us regardless of our circumstances.

We are confronted by both peril and promise on our journey of faith.

Every step of our personal journeys are steadied by drawing from His abiding *presence,* His unrelenting *protection,* and His comprehensive *provision.* His commitment to concern Himself with all that concerns us is proven and unmatched. Even when we wander, He remains the same toward us. He stays true to who He is.

This psalm not only assures and comforts us concerning all we face in the now season of our lives but gives us real hope for what we will face in the future, down the road. Sometimes life can come at us hard but the promise of Jesus is that both goodness and mercy will accompany us *all* the days of our lives!

The Lord is my Shepherd. I shall not want, and I will not be afraid!

I hope you enjoy what you read!

Grace and blessings,
Pastor Marshall Townsley

[1]The Lord is my shepherd;
I shall not want.
[2] He makes me to lie down in green pastures;
He leads me beside the still waters.
[3] He restores my soul;
He leads me in the paths of righteousness
For His name's sake.

[4]Yea, though I walk through the valley of the shadow of death,
I will fear no evil;
For You are with me;
Your rod and Your staff, they comfort me.

[5]You prepare a table before me in the presence of my enemies;
You anoint my head with oil;
My cup runs over.

[6] Surely goodness and mercy shall
follow me
All the days of my life;
And I will dwell in the house of the Lord
Forever.

Psalm 23

1

THE 23RD PSALM: AN ORIGINAL INTERPRETIVE VERSION

THE LORD [A]

- The Creator and Owner of all that can be called alive and living
- The Almighty God, who is Love and lives to love
- Stronger than all
- Wiser without exception
- Supremely compassionate and capable

- Committed and faithful to a thousand generations and beyond

IS MY SHEPHERD [B]

- A one-of-a-kind owner, manager, and husband
- Whose oversight is moment-by-moment and endless
- He knows my name and I love, recognize, and acknowledge His voice
- He sacrificed and laid down His life for me
- He still intercedes for me without pause
- I will follow Him to the ends of the earth
- He has welcomed me, I know acceptance
- I am His and He is mine

I SHALL NOT WANT [C]

- I will not lack in proper care or management
- His care is so complete and thorough I have no need to fear

- I am perfectly content
- I am simply satisfied

HE MAKES ME LIE DOWN [D] IN GREEN PASTURES [E]

- They are so rare in the region
- He has worked selflessly, going before me to cultivate the land so that the "milk flow" and the "honey flow" are heavy, a land of rich, green, luxuriant places to feed
- I know where my next meal is coming from. He never fails to provide
- In flourishing fields, knee deep in grass, I can fill up quickly then lie down quietly to rest and think on His goodness

HE LEADS ME BESIDE THE STILL WATERS [F]

- I drink from the fresh dew of the morning or from the streams that meander through the fields

- My shepherd also takes me to the secret places, too, great rooms chiseled out of the rocks with ramps that lead to fountains where cool, clear, and clean waters flow continually
- In Him, by Him, and through Him I find living water that quenches my thirst. The search ends with Him—I will never thirst again
- I am amazed! Even when it comes to my most basic needs, those essential to survival—food and water—He makes the most of providing me with the best of both
- His care is overwhelming and extravagant

HE RESTORES MY SOUL [G]

- When I find myself in a helpless place, more times than not the result of my own misguided choices, it does not matter to Him; He finds His way to me, rushing to my aid
- He is constantly watching

- He's always aware of where I am and what I am doing. His ears are attentive to my cry
- I know He will hear me and attend carefully to me until I am back on my feet, steady, moving forward once again
- He rescues me again and again

FURTHERMORE, HE LEADS ME IN THE RIGHT PATHS [H]

- Because I belong to Him, He takes the outcome of my life personally
- Left to myself and my own choices without His guidance, I end up separated from the life He provides
- I've proven time and again I don't belong in the lead. He is the Leader, I am the follower. Other voices urge me to go where they want to go and to do as they say. They only think they know the way.
- He sees the big picture and has a plan for me that I must see and obey—my times

are in His hands and I want to be where He is when we finish this journey

- He can be trusted; He knows the way and is the Way!

YES, EVEN THOUGH I WALK THROUGH THE VALLEY OF THE SHADOW OF DEATH; I WILL FEAR NO EVIL; [I] FOR YOU ARE ALWAYS THERE WITH ME AND YOU ARE FOR ME [J]

- I know the time is coming again, the season is near, to move to higher ground
- You want me to grow and increase my capacity for fullness
- Though this is a way well known to You, it is a real challenge for me
- More than just a change in location, it is a strong challenge to my soul
- I can be a little skittish anyway about change, but the shadows of uncertainty

cast even on this well-planned path can be overwhelming

- Add to that the counter plans and strategies of our enemies, who work their evil against us and who lurk in those shadows ready to pounce, and it's understandable why this time of year is so unsettling—certainly not among my favorites!
- But this I have learned. You are always with me from the beginning of this journey to its end and everywhere in between
- Even when darkness is on every side and death's shadows seem to cover all, I will not be afraid
- I am more convinced of Your protective love than the threat of harm or death
- With all I've learned along the way, trusting You is my greatest gain
- I know if I stay close to You, you will bring me out of the uncertainty and intimidation on life's way into the steady warmth of Your light

- You will always complete in me what You begin—that's just the way You are

YOUR ROD AND YOUR STAFF, [K] THEY COMFORT ME [L]

- Your Word to me is powerful, and You are quick to use it on my behalf
- I've never heard or seen anything like it, nothing compares
- When You speak, the darkness flees—it is put on its heels and then runs in stark terror
- When Your Word is declared, there is no other recourse—the final Word has been spoken
- By it my enemies are subdued; they are paralyzed and cannot move
- Even the most brilliant are shown to be fools
- Those with great cunning, who deceive and seduce are exposed and made to run for their very lives

- Before they can strike they are made to fear
- The skillful use of Your Word leaves them completely undone
- Your Word will find its target without exception—bull's-eye again! And it will always accomplish its purpose
- Your Word has conquered and made me more than a conqueror. Who can stand against us?
- Your Word clears the way for me
- By it, I remain on this narrow path safely on my way to experience the higher life in You
- When I consider going astray, when I become headstrong and attempt to set out on my own, it is Your Word that brings me back into Your presence
- Your Word is my wake-up call!
- My judgments and decisions count for nothing apart from the words You speak
- By Your Word I am kept safe and secure

- Where would I be without the presence of the Holy Spirit?
- He is as You are—another Comforter
- By Him I am not only urged but empowered to abide
- By the Holy Spirit, I am kept clean and free! By Your careful, compassionate, examination and counsel, I am healthy and strong
- It's not always easy to be pulled out or aside, but it's always beneficial
- It is by Your Spirit that I am shown things to come, things that await me on this long journey
- By Him You cause me to lift up my head and look ahead and hope
- And should I begin to leave that hope behind, He reminds me of what You see for my life and urges me back to Your loving touch, to obedience and to following after You
- Your touch is not only reassuring, it is essential to my survival and arrival

- Your abiding touch is more than external, it warms me within
- No one else or anything else can touch that part of me
- Your abiding presence makes me fearless and to want to chase life with joy and passion
- Life just wouldn't be the same without You. For that matter, it wouldn't be life at all!

YOU PREPARE A TABLE BEFORE ME IN THE PRESENCE OF MINE ENEMIES; [M] YOU ANOINT MY HEAD WITH OIL [N]

- There is violence all around; the world is a broken place with broken people
- Unseen forces bringing pain and the fear of more
- Enslaving influences promising life but delivering death

- The hopelessness is real, blinding me at times to the future You so thoughtfully have planned for me
- They work unceasingly to make my faith in You a thing of the past
- You, Lord, are my Hiding Place!
- When I am about to be overcome or so it seems, You step in—my powerful Protector and compassionate committed Caretaker!
- You call me aside; You set a divine perimeter about me; Your Word, Your Spirit, Your name and glory keep me
- My enemies can only watch as miracles flow into my life; You have said, "Look, but do not touch!"
- By the anointing I am made whole and my enemies are once again defeated
- I feel renewed as if You had poured Your own strength within me
- Nothing escapes You. Your skillful care and personal attention have brought complete healing and deliverance

- I see it! There is always a special place that You hold in Your heart for me
- It is a place where the weak are made strong. Where the troubled are made to rest. A place where the greatest need is swallowed up by Your grace. And my enemies are made envious by Your care and made to fear—they dare not cross the line
- I'll say it again. You are my Hiding Place and refuge, that special place in the presence of my enemies!

MY CUP IS RUNNING OVER. [O] **SURELY GOODNESS AND MERCY WILL FOLLOW ME ALL THE DAYS OF MY LIFE.** [P] **AND I WILL DWELL IN THE HOUSE OF THE LORD FOREVER.** [Q]

- Your supply is overflowing and endless
- I am living life large as You intended

- I am assured that Your guiding goodness and door-opening mercies will accompany me every step of the way
- I have no other place in all the world that I would rather be than in Your presence, following after You
- And why wouldn't I? No one lives like You live. You stand alone! In a class all by Yourself
- I have nowhere to go or anything to do that's more pressing. Everything else pales by comparison
- Let's go. I'm ready, now. You've won my heart!
- Just being with You is more than enough.
- In You I have found all that is valuable and worthwhile. No reason to wonder or wander any longer
- I came face-to-face with life at its best when I came face-to-face with You

- This is forever and my soul has found perfect peace and I am at rest!

THE LORD IS MY SHEPHERD—I SHALL NOT WANT!

2

EXPLORING GOD'S NAMES AND WORDS

THE LORD [A]

The Hebrew word for LORD is YHWH. YHWH represents the Hebrew letters "Yud-Heh-Vav-Heh."

YHWH is considered the name of the only true God. It is *not* a name bestowed by another but one God chose for Himself.

YHWH is probably pronounced "Yahweh," and means "I Am That I Am." The implication is that God is completely self-sufficient.

It is, therefore, a name that brings emphasis to His unequaled, unrivaled, and unparalleled place in all the universe—all else being created and dependent on Him for their existence.

David seems overwhelmed that someone so great could take interest in someone so small.

He is likely expressing the same wonder that he expresses in Psalm 8, written the same year (1015 BC).

Psalmist David was not only taken by YHWH's unrivaled greatness but also by His personal interest in the man He created.

PSALM 8:3-4 (TPT)

> 3 Look at the splendor of your skies,
> your creative genius glowing in the heavens.
> When I gaze at your moon and your stars,
> mounted like jewels in their settings,
> I know you are the fascinating artist who fashioned it all!

But when I look up and see
such wonder and workmanship above,
I have to ask you this question:

4 Compared to all this cosmic glory,
why would you bother with puny, mortal man
or be infatuated with Adam's sons.

⋆ *Grazing Point.* Lordship is not hardship and communicates the idea of protective cover, not demanding control. It is beneficial not back-breaking. Nor is it ever harsh but healthy. In a military sense, lordship indicates the first one into battle and the last to leave. And scriptures teach that the way of the Lord will always lead to fullness, not famine. Lordship is desirous—not disastrous!

IS MY SHEPHERD [B]

The word most commonly used for *shepherd* in the Hebrew language is *ra'ah*. It is one of the redemptive names by which God revealed

Himself to Israel, each revealing a certain aspect of who God is by nature and essence.

The following are the seven commonly accepted redemptive names of the LORD:

1. Jehovah-Rapha, The Lord our Healer
2. Jehovah-Nissi, the Lord our Banner [or Refuge]
3. Jehovah-Shammah, the Lord (who) is Present
4. Jehovah-Tsidkenu, the Lord our Righteousness
5. Jehovah-Shalom, the Lord our Peace
6. Jehovah-Jireh, the Lord our Provider
7. Jehovah-Ra'ah, the Lord our Shepherd

I am told *ra'ah* is also the Hebrew word for "best friend." David considered Him both LORD and friend. He delighted in calling him by His name as revealed in footnote A above.

It's important to emphasize these names don't just refer to what He provides but who He is by nature. These names are not what He puts on and takes off like a set of clothes.

It is His essence to care and pursue friendship!

★ *Grazing Point.* Never let anyone else be to you what you will not allow or expect God to be. It's not fair to them or you. No one can be God—not even on their best day. No substitutes allowed!

I SHALL NOT WANT [C]

In the Hebrew text, the word *want* means to lack or be lacking, to diminish or decrease.

The well-being of any flock hinged on the care and attention provided by their owner. Sheep were not known for their self-care habits.

Without proper care and provision the sheep were left to forage for themselves. Brown fields and impoverished pastures, shortages in winter, polluted waters, and the real threat of becoming the prey of dogs, cougars, wolves, and rustlers were all they could look forward to.

Though the good shepherd could not keep his sheep from being confronted by all the trouble of the journey or its challenges, through proven, consistent, thoughtful care and management he made certain the flock wanted for nothing.

The apostle Paul couldn't find enough superlatives to describe the generosity of the Father and His commitment to those who trust in Him when he wrote these words by inspiration of the Holy Spirit:

EPHESIANS 3:20 (TPT)

> 20 Never doubt God's mighty power to work in you and accomplish all this. He will achieve infinitely more than your greatest request, your most unbelievable dream, and exceed your wildest imagination! He will outdo them all, for his miraculous power constantly energizes you.

Because the LORD is our Shepherd, as Christians we are confident that we have *all* things that pertain to life as God intends for us, including His full attention!

★ *Grazing Point.* It was Benjamin Franklin who said, "Contentment makes poor men rich; discontent makes rich men poor." Paul wrote to Timothy, "Godliness with contentment is great gain" (1 Timothy 6:6).

HE MAKES ME LIE DOWN [D]

It's almost impossible to get sheep to lie down and rest. To do so they need to experience freedom from fear of all sorts, tension among themselves, aggravation from the torment of flies and parasites and hunger. Not surprisingly, only the shepherd can liberate them from their apprehensiveness.

In the Christian's life there is no reason to ever doubt His presence. He never leaves us. We are never forsaken even when feelings and circumstances paint a very different picture.

Choosing to be aware of His presence will consistently dispel the fear, the nagging pain, and the threatening terror of the unknown. Acknowledgment is the key.

PSALM 4:8 (NIV)

8 In peace I will lie down and sleep,
for you alone, LORD,
make me dwell in safety.

★ *Grazing Point.* We live in an unsettled place. Everywhere we look something is moving or changing. Being anxious about it is understandable but not profitable. Corrie Ten Boom said, "Worry does not empty tomorrow of its sorrow, it empties today of its strength. Never be afraid to trust an unknown future to a known God." Love that!

IN GREEN PASTURES [E]

The majority of the recognized sheep countries of the world are very dry, semi-arid areas. For example, Palestine where David wrote this psalm and kept his father's flocks, especially near Bethlehem, is a dry, brownish, sun-burned wasteland.

W. Phillip Keller comments on the idea in his book, *A Shepherd's Look at Psalm 23*, that green pastures were never the result of chance but the product of foresight, hard labor, time, and skill in land use. "Milk flow" and "honey flow" were agricultural terms used to describe just two of the practical outcomes of providing land rich in green, luxuriant pastures. They are terms that described land that had reached its highest productive state. The sheep owner worked tirelessly to provide the best for his flock.

The good shepherd's generous work was done solely with a focus on his sheep's well-being and health. A hungry, ill-fed sheep is ever on his feet, on the move, searching for his next mouthful of forage with the hope of satisfying his gnawing hunger. Such sheep lack spirit, are not at all content and do not thrive. The loving sheep owner longs to see his sheep provided with more than enough so that the sheep can feed quickly, lie down, and flourish.

Christians can be confident that Jesus has held nothing back in providing all the nourishment necessary for us to enjoy a full and lush abundant life—for our spirit, soul and body. His care is incomprehensible and unmatched by all others.

★ *Grazing Point.* There is no better way to describe the life that Jesus wants for mankind than "abundant" (John 10:10). He wants us to join Him and experience life as He does. True prosperity is not found in the things we possess but in who possesses us. Instead of entertaining ways to exempt yourself from it, find ways to enjoy it!

HE LEADS ME BESIDE THE STILL WATERS [F]

Generally speaking, water came from three main sources on the journey—dew on the grass, deep wells hidden in hand-hewn caverns cut from sandstone, or springs and streams.

Sheep are independent creatures. When they're thirsty, they'll find their own way to get water. But if they don't have access to clean water, they might end up drinking from dirty ponds or stagnant water sources. These places can be filled with parasites and other germs that can make them sick or even die.

Only the skilled shepherd knew where the best, life-giving waters were located, and to find them the sheep had to rely on him to have their thirst satisfied and to remain healthy.

So much of human's searching has to do with quenching the thirsting of their parched souls. They have become willing to drink at almost any source with the hope that the ache will come to an end. In most cases the result is a soul made sick with no dream of a better tomorrow.

Jesus, the Good Shepherd, stands ready not only to guide us to the still waters that will genuinely contribute to wholeness and health but also to Himself who, as living water, alone holds eternal life.

★ *Grazing Point.* One of the greatest miracles ever recorded came on the wings of a command to "be still and know that I am God." The parting of the Red Sea was the first of many in the Scripture that would produce the peace that only comes from Jesus. Peace is not the absence of trouble but the result of faith-filled surrender toward God. The Good Shepherd is our Peace!

HE RESTORES MY SOUL [G]

"Cast" or "cast down" described a sheep that had turned over on its back and could not get back on its feet without help. A "cast" sheep was a distressing sight. Keller says, "Lying on its back, its feet in the air, it flayed away frantically struggling to stand up, without success. Sometimes it would bleat out for help, but generally it lies there lashing about in frightened frustration." There's little time to waste in locating and helping the struggling sheep before it dies.

The watchful shepherd wasn't just aware of the number of his sheep as he checked the flock carefully and often throughout the day but for those who were distressed in any way—in particular one that was on its back. Only a hands-on remedy could save the life of the struggling lamb.

Even those who love Jesus the deepest can become deeply distressed in their souls and need restoration. David, a man after God's own heart cried out to God and said:

PSALM 42:11 (NIV)

11 Why, my soul, are you downcast?
Why so disturbed within me?
Put your hope in God….

Our Good Shepherd, though, will not leave us cast down, whatever the cause, but delights in bringing help and restoration, helping us to regain our composure until we are once again stable and sure-footed, walking with Him and with our brothers and sisters, once again, in faith.

JOB 33:25-26 (NIV)

25 "let their flesh be renewed like a child's;
let them be restored as in the days of their youth" —

26 then that person can pray to God and find favor with him,
they will see God's face and shout for joy;
he will restore them to full well-being.

* *Grazing Point.* There is a weariness that even the best night's sleep won't cure. The soul needs to be assured and made to feel safe before it can experience the refreshing God provides. The Holy Spirit's comfort accomplishes that in us and increases our capacity for genuine renewal. Our exhaustion is no match for God's power.

FURTHERMORE, HE LEADS ME IN THE RIGHT PATHS [H]

Sheep are not at all discerning. They keep their heads down, mindlessly following the sheep ahead of them doing the same thing!

Left to themselves they will get lost and perish in what seems right to them.

Some sheep exhibit a preference for revisiting the same grazing location repeatedly. Over time, this practice can lead to soil degradation, reducing its suitability as a future food source. Moreover, the repeated grazing can create a breeding ground for diseases that can be transmitted to the others. A diligent shepherd is responsible for guiding his flock to fresh grazing areas, keeping them on the move, ensuring their well-being.

Their saving grace is coming to know the voice of their owner and faithfully following him.

To truly enjoy the journey and reach our destination safely, we must become followers of Jesus and be responsive to His lightest whispers.

Success lies in being humble and following Him—actively opposing the stranger's voice but quickly yielding to the voice of Jesus. You might say, "I've never heard His voice." But you have. As a child of God, He is speaking to you through His Spirit. Don't be afraid! In time, you'll start to recognize and discern what He's saying to you. He promised. You are His name's sake—He takes your life experiences personally. No one can be trusted more with the lead.

JOHN 10:2-5 (TPT)

2 But the true Shepherd walks right up to the gate,

3 and because the gatekeeper knows who he is, he opens the gate to let him in. And the sheep recognize the voice of the true Shepherd, for he calls his own by name and leads them out, for they belong to him.

4 And when he has brought out all his sheep, he walks ahead of them and they

> will follow him, for they are familiar with his voice.
>
> 5 But they will run away from strangers and never follow them because they know it's the voice of a stranger.

★ *Grazing Point.* Learning to love His voice is paramount to enjoying relationship with Jesus on the highest level. Jesus is committed to you and growing your relationship with Him. He will speak to you in a way that you can understand. Match His commitment to speak to you with a similar commitment to hear and follow.

YES, EVEN THOUGH I WALK THROUGH THE VALLEY OF THE SHADOW OF DEATH, I WILL FEAR NO EVIL [1]

Here the psalmist is likely referring to the ravines and gorges that must be navigated on the upward summer trek into the alpine meadows above the timberline in the summer.

These steep-sided valleys were filled with uncertainty. Rockslides, poisonous plants, the ravages of predators and unpredictable and sudden changes in the weather were common.

The best way to the top was always along these valleys because of the gradual grades.

It's worth noting that nothing took the seasoned shepherd by surprise. He was fully prepared to safeguard and tend his sheep with all he possessed under every circumstance. They had no reason to fear!

Likewise, Christians have no reason to be afraid on their faith journey to a higher experience in Christ. There should be no mysterious message attached to the valley experience as many believers tend to do. "What is God trying to teach me? Why did He allow this to happen?" etc. It's just part of the landscape and the process of spiritual growth.

We live in a broken world with broken people. This is not heaven and we shouldn't expect it to be. Doing so only adds to the frustration and confusion we often feel as Christians. Our Shepherd doesn't create trouble for us only to become the one who delivers us from it. He doesn't make us sick only to heal us. Nor does He make us poor only then to prosper us. He doesn't dig a ditch simply to fill it. Those are made-up misrepresentations of who Jesus is and how He operates. His unquestionable care for us should assure us and cast out *all* fear.

PSALM 56:9-11 (TPT)

9 The very moment I call to you for a father's help

the tide of battle turns and my enemies
flee.
This one thing I know: God is on my
side!

10 I trust in the Lord. And I praise him!
I trust in the Word of God. And I
praise him!

11 What harm could man do to me?
With God on my side I will not be
afraid of what comes.
My heart overflows with praise to God
and for his promises.
I will always trust in him.

* *Grazing Point.* Following Jesus is fraught with distractions galore. Some things threaten us—others are alluring. We must keep our gaze set on Jesus at all times and ever be listening for the sound of His voice. The Holy Spirit is your Teacher in all things. Charles Spurgeon said, "Faith is the gaze of a soul upon a saving God." Keep your gaze raised.

FOR YOU ARE ALWAYS THERE WITH ME AND YOU ARE FOR ME

It's worth noting that the narrative changes here. The psalmist goes from talking *about* the Shepherd to *speaking to* Him directly. Being aware of Jesus' presence is always essential and indispensable in matters of peace and stability, even more so when we are faced with our greatest challenges. David found great comfort throughout his own journey of faith in knowing that God was with Him and on His side. How much more should the child of God indulge in doing the same!

PSALM 27:4 (TPT)

> 4 Here's the one thing I crave from Yahweh,
> the one thing I seek above all else:
> I want to live with him every moment in his house,
> Beholding the marvelous beauty of Yahweh,

filled with awe, delighting in his glory
and grace.
I want to contemplate in his temple.

I want to live my life so close to Him that He takes pleasure in my every prayer.

★ *Grazing Point.* If God is for you, shouldn't you be? If Jesus is on your side and pulling for you, stop being your worst enemy! Stop speaking negatively about yourself or doubting your worth. Walk in confidence knowing that Jesus is cheering you on. God didn't need to be convinced to love you or keep company with you. Nor is He looking to find a reason to stop. Learn how to daily pray in His presence.

YOUR ROD AND YOUR STAFF [K]

I had the chance to visit shepherds in their fields in Romania, and I was amazed by how little they carry with them. They travel super light! One of them gave me his staff, and I noticed right away that it didn't fit my hand. He then reached for my hand, held it up to his, and compared the two. Even though we didn't speak the same language, he still managed to tell me that the equipment shepherds carry have to be custom-made. Customized equipment works best when used by experienced and skilled people—not by someone who's just an admiring amateur. The tools they usually carry were a young sapling that had been carved to form a knob-kerri or rod, and a long, thin stick or staff.

The rod became his main weapon of defense for himself and for his sheep. It came to symbolize his power and his authority in any situation, especially those that were threatening.

The rod should be thought of as God's Word. When He speaks, the final word has been spoken.

ECCLESIASTES 8:4

4 Where the word of a king is, there
is power;
And who may say to him, "What are
you doing?"

ECCLESIASTES 8:4 (MSG)

> 4 The king has the last word. Who dares say to him, "What are you doing?"

When Jesus was confronted personally by Satan in the wilderness, He drew His strength from the written Word of the Father and declared it against His enemy. Every believer should be encouraged to do likewise and to expect a similar outcome.

The staff is unique to shepherding. No one working any other job in the world carries a shepherd's staff. Just as the rod is typical of authority, so the staff is emblematic of his company. The sheep take great comfort in being reminded that he is ever with them and within his reach.

For Christians, the staff Jesus wields is a reminder of His constant presence and everlasting commitment to our relationship. We are never alone and have no fear of being abandoned.

HEBREWS 13:5 (AMPC)

> 5 …for He [God] Himself has said, I will not in any way fail you nor give you up nor leave you without support. [I will] not, [I will] not, [I will] not in any degree leave you helpless nor forsake nor let [you] down (relax My hold on you)! [Assuredly not!]

He, the Holy Spirit, is the One Jesus said would come after Him to abide within the follower of Jesus. He is, among so many things, our constant reminder that we are never alone and never forsaken. That we are never a mere afterthought of our Good Shepherd, Jesus. He is our constant comfort in an otherwise desolate and distressed world.

He is appropriately called the Comforter—the One who stands closely by and with us.

★ *Grazing Point.* God's Word is always accompanied by the power to fulfill itself. God is actively watching over His Word to perform it. He doesn't obligate Himself to do what we think He said or wish He had said. And just saying God said something doesn't make it so. That's using His name in vain. But what He has promised He also will perform. God's Word and the Spirit always work together to accomplish the will of God.

THEY COMFORT ME [L]

The Hebrew word for *comfort* in this verse is very revealing. It is the word *naham* and it means to breathe strongly toward. It indicates someone who is deeply moved with compassion and sorrow over someone who is hurting or without help. It implies a lending of one's strength in another's time of weakness with the intent of getting them back on their feet and moving past their current dilemma.

Thank God for the constant help of the Spirit of God.

JOHN 14:16-18 (AMPC)

16 And I will ask the Father, and He will give you another Comforter (Counselor, Helper, Intercessor, Advocate, Strengthener, and Standby), that He may remain with you forever—

17 The Spirit of Truth, Whom the world cannot receive (welcome, take to its heart), because it does not see Him or know and recognize Him. But you know and recognize Him, for He lives with you [constantly] and will be in you.

18 I will not leave you as orphans [comfortless, desolate, bereaved, forlorn, helpless]; I will come [back] to you.

The new life that we now possess in Christ can only be fully experienced as we lean more and more on and deepen our daily communion with the Holy Spirit. Jesus wants us to have a relationship with the Spirit that can only be described as a *baptism.* In the first century, the word came to metaphorically describe someone or something that had been fully submerged beneath the surface of the water or immersed in the sea. Josephus used the word to describe the city of Jerusalem being "overwhelmed" or "plunged" into destruction.

The act of baptism was considered both total and transitional. Total in the sense that it involved the whole person and the whole personality of the one being baptized. And transitional in the sense that the one being baptized was passing from one stage or realm of experience into a new one, never previously entered into.

The Christian cannot overestimate the need for the help of the Holy Spirit in realizing the new life meant for the new creation.

⋆ *Grazing Point.* Think about this. Every step Peter took walking on the water was done in the strength of the Holy Spirit. He didn't take a single step, big or small, on his own. Without God's help, it was either sink or swim. Christians have a bad habit of beginning their walk depending on God only to transition their trust to themselves or somewhere else. Learn to trust in Jesus—start to finish. What He begins He *also* will finish.

YOU PREPARE A TABLE BEFORE ME IN THE PRESENCE OF MINE ENEMIES [M]

The word *table* used here refers to the high, flat-topped plateaus so much sought after by shepherds for their time in the mountain country during the summer with their flocks.

These areas are intended to be places of rest and recovery after taxing climbs. They are necessary stops to insure the overall health of the sheep during what can be a demanding and rigorous trek.

To insure the best experience for those following him, the thoughtful shepherd had already visited these areas, going before the sheep preparing for their stay. He is careful to know the lay of the land before the first one arrives. The good shepherd had already cleaned out the water holes, springs, and drinking places for those he led. He has done the hard work of removing poisonous plants and other harmful vegetation that might harm or sicken the flock in any way. This is part of his overall plan for grazing during their stay.

Their safety is also of primary concern while staying out in the open. Predators are known to watch from the surrounding high cliffs hoping for an opportunity to prey on the innocent and especially those who might stray from the group.

The shepherd familiarizes himself with any footprints or signs of the ever-present dangers of cougars, wolves, coyotes, and bears hoping for a swift attack. It is only his preparation for such an eventuality that can possibly save a sheep from being panicked and slaughtered by their predators.

The message is clear for believers. Our Shepherd wants to preempt any disaster for those He loves. He wants our times in the high country to be enjoyed in peace—perfect peace. And we will be at peace if we have the sense to draw near and stay near Him where He can protect us. Following the One who is wisdom to us (1 Corinthians 1:30) can be the difference as we travel among our enemies. And if we are suddenly surprised by the thief, we can be certain that there is One who fights for us who has overcome all the world. We can be confident that He will bring help, healing, restoration, and recovery.

PSALM 91:2-3

> 2 I will say of the LORD, "He is my refuge and my fortress;
> My God, in Him I will trust."
>
> 3 Surely He shall deliver you from the snare of the fowler
> And from the perilous pestilence.

Psalm 91:9-16

9 Because you have made the LORD, who is my refuge,
Even the Most High, your dwelling place,

10 No evil shall befall you,
Nor shall any plague come near your dwelling;

11 For He shall give His angels charge over you,
To keep you in all your ways.

12 In their hands they shall bear you up,
Lest you dash your foot against a stone.

13 You shall tread upon the lion and the cobra,
The young lion and the serpent you shall trample underfoot.

14 "Because he has set his love upon Me, therefore I will deliver him;

I will set him on high, because he has
known My name.

15 He shall call upon Me, and I will
answer him;
I will be with him in trouble;
I will deliver him and honor him.

16 With long life I will satisfy him,
And show him My salvation."

★ *Grazing Point.* We happen to enjoy the distinct advantage of having the Leader who not only provides the best in thoughtful oversight but unmatched foresight as well. Hindsight works to explain the mistake. Oversight sorts it out. And foresight prevents it (Proverbs 22:3).

YOU ANOINT MY HEAD WITH OIL [N]

Keller says, "In the words of the experienced sheepman that summer time is fly time." Hordes of insects emerge with the arrival of warm weather. Their attacks on the sheep can turn from constant aggravation to deadly if they go unchecked.

Of particular significance is the nose or nasal fly. These small flies hover around the heads of the sheep seeking to lay their eggs in the soft membranes of their noses. If they are successful, the hatched larvae make their way further up into the nasal passage and burrow into the flesh causing intense pain and inflammation. Sheep have been known to take their own lives because of the constant irritation.

Another enemy threatening the overall health of the flock was scab. Scab is a very contagious disease most often transmitted from one sheep to the other as they rubbed their heads together. For the Hebrew people, the presence of scab was a major consideration when examining a lamb deemed for sacrifice. Remember a sacrifice lamb had to be without spot or blemish.

The preemptive remedy for both of these infestations was a special blend of olive oil mixed with sulfur and spices. The timely and consistent application of this oil mix was enough to prevent disease and its spread and ward off the attacks of the many small, winged adversaries.

As Christians, we have literally been "smeared" with oil in our inner self. The King James Version of the Bible uses the word *anointed.* We can never overstate the importance of the Holy Spirit's presence and ministry in our journey of faith. Jesus lovingly assured His disciples that they would not be left without comfort and peace upon His departure. He offered them the surest of promises concerning the coming Holy Spirit and His personal touch and ministry to each of them. He says in John 14:

JOHN 14:26 (AMPC)

> 26 But the Comforter (Counselor, Helper, Intercessor, Advocate, Strengthener, Standby), the Holy Spirit, Whom the Father will send in My name [in My place, to represent Me and act on

> My behalf], He will teach you all things. And He will cause you to recall (will remind you of, bring to your remembrance) everything I have told you.

The Holy Spirit continues to make Jesus real to us, every day reminding us of all He has spoken and done for us—encouraging and building a greater trust and confidence in Him. Thoughtfully given and assigned to each of us, the Holy Spirit deserves a special place of honor and attention as we follow Him moving forward. His leadership is unequaled. The urging of the apostles was to grow and establish rich communion with Him. His daily assignment from Jesus is to help us.

The opportunity to live in the power of His strength and might is the difference maker in every circumstance for us who believe. His supply is more than enough to meet every challenge along the way.

* *Grazing Point.* The challenges of following Jesus can be overwhelming. A single misleading

thought in the mind, like a single fly, can produce the worst of outcomes. But the Holy Spirit's care is so rigorous and detailed that we are never without the grace to overcome. He is always in attendance and available, able and up to the task. He is amenable or willing—active and committed. He is our Best Forever Friend.

MY CUP IS RUNNING OVER ○

"My cup" was an often-used phrase at the time this psalm was written to refer to one's destiny or fortune in life. I can picture David making every effort to find words to summarize all that he has previously expressed as he closes this psalm. He is simply taken and overwhelmed by the Good Shepherd's over-the-top, always more-than-enough, thoughtful care and unquestionable love for His people.

As Christians, we can readily say that our cup runs over because Christ poured out His life and continues to do so without hesitation for us! His supply is exceedingly, abundantly, above all that we could ever ask or imagine to ask.

As we receive from the communion table and drink from Messiah's cup, we're reminded of His selfless act of emptying Himself so that we could join Him in life, both here and into eternity.

When Jesus says He came to give us life, it means that what we had wasn't really life. As the apostle Paul writes, we were "dead in our sins and trespasses," completely separated from the God kind of life.

Jesus describes that life as an abundant one.

JOHN 10:10 (AMPC)

> 10 The thief comes only in order to steal and kill and destroy. I came that they may have and enjoy life, and have it in abundance (to the full, till it overflows).

Jesus says in another place,

LUKE 12:32 (AMPC)

> 32 Do not be seized with alarm and struck with fear, little flock, for it is your Father's good pleasure to give you the kingdom!

There's not a cup sizable enough to hold all that the Good Shepherd has made ours!

* *Grazing Point.* Ron Adams, son of Billie Adams, said, "If all we got was what we deserved we would be in a world of hurt." The riches of God's grace toward us has made us rich, by God's standards, in all things. We should never apologize for the *all* that He has provided. Just the opposite. We should boast in Him and what He has accomplished. "Thank you" never seems enough for the "more than enough" He has made available to us. But it's a great start!

SURELY GOODNESS AND MERCY WILL FOLLOW ME ALL THE DAYS OF MY LIFE [P]

In ancient literature, sheep were referred to as "those of the golden hooves" because they were regarded and esteemed so highly for their beneficial affect on the land they traveled through. Where previously there had been only poverty and deplorable waste, there now followed flourishing fields of rich abundance.

The well-managed sheep left behind something worthwhile, productive, beautiful and beneficial for both themselves and others who followed—fertile, weed-free, beautiful abundance. In other words, goodness and mercy had followed the flock.

Goodness can only be described by what we see in Jesus. We all have an opinion, but there is none good but God. That goodness flows to us not because we could ever deserve or merit it. It is a beautiful portion of the saving grace that has been given to us. It's that goodness that turns us away from evil and toward following after Jesus. His goodness is a constant reminder that this full life is a gift, and we must never take it for granted.

Mercies are new every morning. Mercy is God sparing me from what I deserve and creating a new opportunity to make things right. A new sunrise, a fresh start to the day, a chance to move past my latest failure to dream again about my future. Both mercy and grace are essential to living life as God intends. Mercy creates a new opportunity and grace enables me to make the most of it!

HEBREWS 4:16 (AMPC)

> 16 Let us then fearlessly and confidently and boldly draw near to the throne of grace (the throne of God's unmerited favor to us sinners), that we may receive mercy [for our failures] and find grace to help in good time for every need [appropriate help and well-timed help, coming just when we need it].

Beyond experiencing His guiding goodness, door-opening mercies, and grace-supplied exploits, a legacy of His goodness is established for generations to come.

* *Grazing Point.* It's really encouraging to know that the undeserved, unmerited blessing that we possess in Christ is not only sustainable but transmittable. We have often heard that we are "blessed to be a blessing." When you find yourself blessed, immediately respond with an open hand to share it with others. Those who are before us are every bit as important as those we leave behind. Leave a legacy of generosity instead of avarice and greed. Make things "golden" for the next generation.

AND I WILL DWELL IN THE HOUSE OF THE LORD FOREVER

There's no place like home. You can see it in their body language and demeanor. Here they will find rest and renewal before they set out on their next journey and next series of challenges. But their peace doesn't return by reason of familiar surroundings alone. The sight of a well-known face, their faithful shepherd, is paramount. Once again, the one who went before them to prepare the way, the one who was with them every step of the journey has now finished alongside of them. His presence is a constant reminder of an unrelenting commitment and care for them. They are at home *with* him.

They have no reason to wander. All they could possibly need or desire is right here, at home, with him.

Jesus never considers life without us. He doesn't look for a way out even when things aren't as they should be. Nor does He flee when things go bad. When Adam and Eve sinned in the Garden, it wasn't God Who hid Himself—they did. God's first move was toward them to make a way back. Salvation has some beautiful theological points to be made; but in its simplest form, salvation is fixing a relationship that went terribly wrong.

Jesus made it possible for all people to come home. And for those of us who have made the decision to follow Him as the Lord our Shepherd, there is no greater love or life to be experienced. There are no viable alternatives to compare to the peace of being at home with and in Him!

ROMANS 8:31-32 (TPT)

31 So, what does all this mean? If God has determined to stand with us, tell me, who then could ever stand against us?

32 For God has proved his love by giving us his greatest treasure, the gift of his Son. And since God freely offered him up as the sacrifice for us all, he certainly won't withhold from us anything else he has to give.

ROMANS 8:35 (TPT)

35 Who could ever separate us from the endless love of God's Anointed One? Absolutely no one! For nothing in the

> universe has the power to diminish his love toward us. Troubles, pressures, and problems are unable to come between us and heaven's love. What about persecutions, deprivations, dangers, and death threats? No, for they are all impotent to hinder omnipotent love,

ROMANS 8:39 (TPT)

> 39 There is no power above us or beneath us—no power that could ever be found in the universe that can distance us from God's passionate love, which is lavished upon us through our Lord Jesus, the Anointed One!

Our good Shepherd, Jesus, has been faithful in the past, He is right now watching over His Word to perform it in the present, and He will be faithful to the end for generations to come.

There is no greater comfort than knowing you are fully known and fully loved by Jesus.

Sheila Walsh, noted Christian vocalist, songwriter, evangelist, author, and inspirational speaker said, "Peace is not the absence of trouble, but the presence of Christ." All that was lost through Adam's fall and more has been recovered in Christ. There really is no place like home.

★ *Grazing Point.* Nothing compares to the enduring acceptance that we find in Jesus. There is nothing temporary about His genuine, unconditional love for you personally. As difficult as it is to grasp, God doesn't love us because we are all so lovable. He loves us because of Who He is. As startling as it may be, God never asked you to qualify for it. Who would have thought it would be so difficult to receive a free gift!

3

A Few Final Thoughts

On September 28, 2024, my wife and I were awakened by an unfamiliar sound.

We had just welcomed dear friends from Arizona into our home for a special church event that weekend. After dinner, we decided to go to bed early, as Saturday would be busy with more guests coming for a casual get together.

Between 3 and 4 a.m., a loud, roaring noise woke us from a deep sleep. I jumped out of bed and found the source—a small intercom speaker installed in the north wall of our bedroom. I turned it off, but the noise persisted from the kitchen where the main unit was.

I put on clothes and made my way to the other end of the house to disable the other unit. As I walked up the hallway, I smelled an electrical fire! It was unmistakable. I turned to the right and went into the guest bathroom only a few feet away.

I looked up and saw the plastic white grille on the exhaust fan melting onto the floor and surrounding areas, including the tub. A hole had been burned in the fabric shower curtain, but it hadn't spread. There was no smoke in the room, as it had been contained above the fan between the ceiling and the roof. The house's fire alarms, including the one across the hall, were all functional and hadn't been set off. I could see the fire's glow and knew we had to act immediately. The fan had malfunctioned and overheated.

This was my first time experiencing a structure fire much less attempting to put one out. I remembered where the fire extinguisher was and grabbed it from the garage. I pulled the handle, pointed it at the fire 10 feet above me, and pulled it. The fire seemed to go out. I fired again just to be sure.

Cindi arrived, and our guests gathered in the hallway to see what was happening. I was on the bathroom floor cleaning up and explaining when I heard a soft pop. I looked up and saw the fire had reignited! I picked up the extinguisher, attempted to fire it again but it had no pressure.

We called Albuquerque Fire and Rescue immediately and we all prayed. After a short wait, they arrived. They were wonderful, ensuring everyone was out of the house and in good health. They showed up with flashing lights and a team to handle any remaining fire or electrical threats. After about an hour and a half, they concluded all was good. The damage was minimal and contained. They didn't need much water and limited opening the ceiling to a small 27' x 30" area. Much of the existing installation above and around the area had to be removed for the sake of precaution.

"Truly, it could have been much worse," the fire marshal said. He praised our calmness, clear thinking, and quick actions for the outcome. We thanked them and thanked God for them as they drove away. Early morning gave way to the new day, the neighborhood quiet and for the most part seemed still asleep.

We spent the rest of the day cleaning and preparing for the party—thinking and talking about the details of what had just happened. We rejoiced in God's undeniable care. It truly could have had such a different outcome were it not for the Good Shepherd's presence, protection, and provision.

HIS PRESENCE

From the sudden, forceful awakening by the blaring speakers, I experienced God's peace. How is that possible?

On my faith journey, I've learned that Jesus' peace is supernatural, different from the world's peace. He says,

> Peace I leave with you, My peace I give you; not as the world gives do I give to you. Let not your heart be troubled, neither let it be afraid.
>
> John 14:27 (NKJV)

You can possess this peace and it can possess you, even in chaos. It's a spiritual force that brings order where disorder reigns.

You can *experience* this peace and *exercise* it.

It's so powerful that we're taught to let it lead or rule our hearts when overwhelmed or unsettled.

> And let the peace (soul harmony which comes) from Christ rule (act as umpire continually) in your hearts [deciding and settling with finality all questions that arise in your minds, in that peaceful state] to which as [members of Christ's] one body you were also called [to live]. And be thankful (appreciative), [giving praise to God always].
>
> Colossians 3:15 (AMPC)

As I processed my circumstances, I experienced a soundness of mind and a quiet calm. My steps were ordered, and I knew my final outcome would be good.

I see peace as God's certainty. If I follow Him, His certainty about all things becomes mine.

I hope this helps you as it has me. The Good Shepherd won't just *talk* you through something; He'll *walk* you through it!

HIS PROTECTION

The intercom system that hadn't been in use for years acted as a fire alarm. It wasn't wired, though, to act as one under any circumstances. I thought the wiring might have been damaged causing it to screech at such a high volume. But after we examined all things after the fire, it appeared untouched and operating as it was designed to. That would not have been the case had it been touched by fire.

All four of us were sound asleep in the house when the horrible noise woke us up. If it hadn't, the outcome could have been completely different.

I'm not one to overstate things, but I won't ignore a miracle when I see or experience one either. I believe in miracles and one occurred on that early Saturday morning.

God protected us.

Scripture mentions that God sends angels with special orders to protect us wherever we go, defending us from all harm (see Psalm 91:11 TPT).

In the 23rd Psalm as we have studied, he says:

> Yes, though I walk through the [deep, sunless] valley of the shadow of death, I will fear or dread no evil, for You are with me; Your rod [to protect] and Your staff [to guide], they comfort me.
>
> Psalm 23:4 (AMPC)

We live in a damaged and fragmented world that's becoming more violent and threatening. But as believers, we can be assured that God is our Refuge, our Shelter.

Another favorite psalm of mine is Psalm 27, and verse 5 is my favorite:

> For in the day of trouble He will hide me in His shelter; in the secret place of His tent He will hide me; He will set me high upon a rock.
>
> Psalm 27:5 (AMPC)

Circumstances are unpredictable at best and we don't always experience God's best for our lives. But we should never allow what we experience to shape our interpretation of God's character or His Word to us—a mistake that far too many of us make. We should instead insist that the revelation of God's Word given to us by the Holy Spirit shape what we come to believe. After all, we walk by faith as God's people, not by sight.

> For we live by faith, not by what we see with our eyes.
>
> 2 Corinthians 5:7 (TPT)

The Good Shepherd should have the final say in all things. The information He provides is never misinformation, and His voice always leads to life and victory.

He sees beyond what we see and invites us to always trust Him no matter the present landscape.

His Provision

Whether it was the unexpected wake-up call or the critical wisdom to remember where the fire extinguisher was, to providing repair or bringing comfort to us all—God provided.

In the 42 days that followed, all of our needs—spirit, soul, body and financially—were completely met beyond our expectations.

I was hit hard emotionally later in the day after things settled down as I attempted to focus on things that still needed taken care of before our guests started arriving.

The Holy Spirit rose up within me, and I leaned hard on Him. The comfort and strength

He provided was all I needed. Cindi, my wife, enjoyed the same as did our friends. We pulled together as we had many times before in crisis and were better for it.

As the hours passed I felt invigorated and refreshed.

Over a brief period of time, I made some phone calls for help concerning all the necessary repairs. Once again, the results were more than imagined.

Paul wrote to the church at Ephesus in one place these words concerning what we might expect God to do when we ask for His help:

> Never doubt God's mighty power to work in you and accomplish all this. He will achieve infinitely more than your greatest request, your most unbelievable dream, and exceed your wildest imagination! He will outdo them all, for his miraculous power constantly energizes you.
>
> Ephesians 3:20 (TPT)

All of the repair work was provided by my Christian friends—all experts in their fields—in a timely fashion and without personal cost to us! They refused to be paid.

Anyone who has lived any life at all knows how expensive materials and labor have become. Yet, within weeks you would never had known there had been a fire in our home. And it would have been even sooner had we been in town and not traveling during the weeks that followed the incident. No evidence, not even an odor, remained. Praise God for His provision!

"*I shall not want!*" David declared, pointing to the goodness and faithfulness of the Good Shepherd. His calm, faith-filled words continued to flow from his lips as he writes:

> Surely or only goodness, mercy, and unfailing love shall follow me all the days of my life, and through the length of my days the house of the Lord [and His presence] shall be my dwelling place.
>
> Psalm 23:6 (AMPC)

The resources He has are far beyond ours. Whatever circumstances you face, He has seen the need, gone before you and provided more than enough to help. He's boundless and His supply is boundless. His goodness is in hot pursuit not just today but every day.

If you are feeling down, I encourage you to lift your head up. He'll even help you with that! I hope you know how deeply committed He is to caring for you in every way. What you see now isn't all there is. There are a ton of "sometime things" that we have to deal with but we can never forget the "unchanging things" that our Good Shepherd has provided for us.

> Jesus, the Anointed One, is always the same—yesterday, today, and forever.
>
> Hebrews 13:8 (TPT)

I'm sensing right now as I finish writing, the need to pray for you…

4

A Prayer for You

Father God,

I pray today, first for a ***return****, if need be, to Your lordship and our privileged place of following closely after You. You offer mercy for new opportunities and grace to help us make the most of them. We receive both mercy and grace now by faith.*

I pray for fresh ***revelation*** *of Your thoughtful provision for every area of our lives, literally every area. As well as for an understanding of the deep commitment*

You have made to get it into our hands for us to enjoy and to use wisely.

I pray for ***relief****, special lifting grace tailored specifically to what's happening now and for the weariness we've carried within.*

I pray for ordained times that will ***restore*** *faith,* ***renew*** *strength, and* ***revive*** *joy.*

I pray that we would ***regain*** *our mental and emotional health. We thank You for deliverance from all that troubles us in our minds, now. We declare a soundness of mind for all, in Jesus' name.*

I also pray for supernatural ***release*** *from what continues to threaten us and fill us with fear. Lord, cause us to recognize and to hear Your voice and to resist any attempts of the stranger, words from the shadows, to get us off path.*

I pray ***rehabilitation*** *concerning our ability to hope again and willingness to dream great things for the future. Open our eyes to how You see us and how* *valuable we are to You and to all You have prepared for us.*

And remind us, Holy Spirit, of the superabundance that we already possess in Christ—a life we could never deserve or afford.

We respond with a heartfelt please and thank You and the assurance that You have both heard and answered our prayer.

In Jesus' exalted name we pray this day, so be it and amen!

5

Meet the Good Shepherd

David learned how to trust God's love and His commitment to care for him over time.

You can do the same. But it all begins by first establishing a relationship with Him if you haven't already done so.

Scripture teaches that we have all sinned and are in need of forgiveness and a change of heart before that can happen. Again, as stated earlier, salvation is about fixing a relationship with God gone bad. We need to be reconciled to Him.

That happens by deciding to follow Jesus as Lord of our lives, for what remains of our lives here and into eternity. We are saved by grace through faith, the Bible says. It is the only offer on the table! If we could earn or merit our place at His table through good works, then grace would not have been necessary.

Christianity's uniqueness is seen in grace. In other faiths and systems of belief the thread of justifying or qualifying ourselves before God through good appears over and again. However, our forgiveness and acceptance with God has never been a matter of *achieving* it but *receiving* it!

And that is what faith does. It is the only way to access the grace of God. That's true at the beginning of your journey of faith and will remain true to its end.

When you decide to become a follower of His, a miracle takes place. It results in you becoming a new you and part of His family, the Church.

Consider this verse:

> Therefore if any person is [ingrafted] in Christ (the Messiah) he is a new creation (a new creature altogether);

> the old [previous moral and spiritual condition] has passed away. Behold, the fresh and new has come!
>
> 2 Corinthians 5:17 (AMPC)

You become new deep inside the moment you sincerely trust in Him. At the same time, the Holy Spirit will come to live inside you and will always be there for you as you learn the walk of faith. You will spend the rest of your life here discovering how to trust God more and come to know the "Jesus Way" to live.

You can pray right now and God will hear you and receive you. He loves you more than you can imagine.

Pray this from your heart. Don't just go through the motions.

> *Dear God in Heaven,*
>
> *Today, I make a no-turning-back decision to submit to Jesus as my Lord, my Savior and Shepherd.*
>
> *I am so grateful for the sacrifice He made at the Cross with me in mind.*

Though He died for my sins, I believe He is now alive because You raised Him from the dead.

I turn from a lifetime of disregarding Him and living independently of Him. I turn from a life marked by sin to follow Jesus without reservation. I hold nothing back.

Thank You for forgiving me and granting me not just a second chance but a brand-new life!

I determine to love You with all of my heart by the help of the Holy Spirit and the grace You provide—to follow You every day, 24/7, for what remains of my life here into eternity.

Thank You so much for loving me so deeply. I love You, too!

In Jesus' name I pray.

Amen!

Now, tell someone. Call, text, email, or just show up at the door of a friend and share that you just made Jesus Lord of your life!

Find a good, life-giving, Spirit-filled church in your area that you can become part of. Make certain that the pastor and the people love the Bible and stay true to the text. Don't get comfortable watching online—it's not the same as personally being there among believers.

And get a Bible if you don't already have one. Start reading with the Gospel of John. Read it over and over again before you branch out to the other Gospels written by Matthew, Mark, and Luke.

From there, read the Acts of the Apostles (the book of Acts), which is so amazing. It reveals the early history, in part, of the growth of God's Family, the Church, and of His Kingdom around the world.

From there, an entire collection of letters written by the leaders of the early churches are written. The teaching and instruction they communicated are just as fitting and suitable for us today. The truth is always the truth. We don't get to define it, but we can certainly discover and live by it.

And, now, by one miraculous act, you have become part of it all. Enjoy living the life you could never deserve from the place of God's grace. I call it the *unaffordable life!*

Congratulations!
So happy for you,
Pastor Marshall

About the Author

Marshall and Cindi Townsley are the founding pastors of Believers Center of Albuquerque. Since founding the church in 1980, Marshall and Cindi have emphasized the grace of God and encouraged believers to rest in God's unchanging character.

In the Right Hands, This Book Will Change Lives!

Most of the people who need this message will not be looking for this book. To change their lives, you need to **put a copy of this book in their hands.**

Our ministry is constantly seeking methods to find the people who need this anointed message to change their lives. **Will you help us reach these people?**

Extend this ministry by sowing three, five, ten, or *even more* books today and change people's lives for the better! Your generosity will be part of catalyzing the Great Awakening that many have been prophesying and praying for.